D1156427

915.1156
B

C.1

GREAT CITIES
OF THE WORLD

BEIJING

NICOLA BARBER

DISCARD

WORLD ALMANAC® LIBRARY

STAUNTON PUBLIC LIBRARY

Please visit our web site at: www.worldalmanaclibrary.com
For a free color catalog describing World Almanac® Library's list of high-quality books
 and multimedia programs, call 1-800-848-2928 (USA) or 1-800-387-3178 (Canada).
World Almanac® Library's fax: (414) 332-3567.

Library of Congress Cataloging-in-Publication Data available upon request from publisher.
Fax (414) 336-0157 for the attention of the Publishing Records Department.

ISBN 0-8368-5028-9 (lib. bdg.)
ISBN 0-8368-5188-9 (softcover)

First published in 2004 by
World Almanac® Library
330 West Olive Street, Suite 100
Milwaukee, WI 53212 USA

Copyright © 2004 by World Almanac® Library.

Produced by Discovery Books
Editor: Kathryn Walker
Series designers: Laurie Shock, Keith Williams
Designer and page production: Keith Williams
Photo researcher: Rachel Tisdale
Maps: Stefan Chabluk
Consultant: Morris Rossabi, Senior Research Scholar, Columbia University
World Almanac® Library editorial direction: Mark J. Sachner
World Almanac® Library editor: Jenette Donovan Guntly
World Almanac® Library art direction: Tammy Gruenewald
World Almanac® Library production: Jessica Morris

Photo credits: AKG-Images: pp. 11, 12, 18; Art Directors & Trip: cover and title page, pp. 15, 24, 39; Art Directors
 & Trip/T. Bognar: p. 17; Chris Fairclough: pp. 22, 25, 29, 31, 36, 43; Corbis: pp. 6, 10, 41; Corbis/Yves Forestier: p. 42;
Corbis/Peter Turnley: p. 13; Hutchison/Melanie Friend: pp. 4, 38; Hutchison/Dr. John Fuller: p. 35; Panos Pictures/Mark
Henley: pp. 28, 32; Popperfoto: p. 27; Still Pictures/Andy Crump: p. 14; Still Pictures/Uniphoto Press International:
 pp. 8, 19, 20, 21, 23, 26, 34, 40

Cover caption: Beijing's most common form of transportation is the bicycle.

All rights reserved. No part of this book may be reproduced, stored in a retrieval system, or transmitted in any form or
by any means, electronic, mechanical, photocopying, recording, or otherwise, without the prior written permission of
the copyright holder.

Printed in the United States of America

1 2 3 4 5 6 7 8 9 08 07 06 05 04

Contents

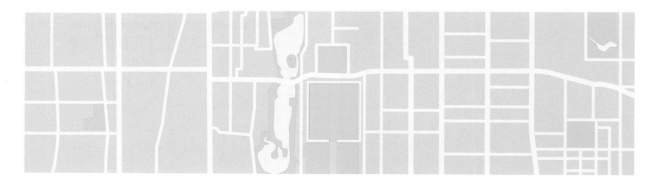

Introduction

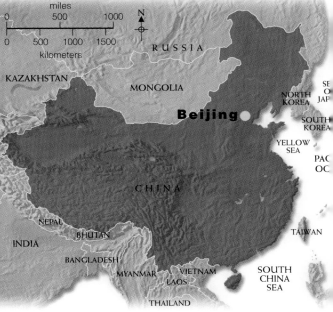

Beijing is the capital of the People's Republic of China. Although it is not the largest city in China (that is Shanghai), Beijing is nevertheless the political and cultural heart of the country. Beijing's status as the capital stretches back many centuries, and the city is home to some of the most famous and historic sites in China, including the Forbidden City, Tiananmen Square, the Temple of Heaven, the Lama Temple, and, to the north, the Great Wall of China.

◀ *Sunlight reflects off of the golden tiled roofs of the former Imperial Palace, also known as the Forbidden City. The palace is located in the heart of Beijing.*

Today, Beijing is a busy, modern city where skyscrapers and high-rise apartment buildings dwarf traditional courtyard houses. People wearing the latest designer-label fashions walk the streets alongside those dressed in traditional "Mao" suits.

Beijing will host the Olympic Games in the summer of 2008, and city planners are busy upgrading Beijing's roads, airports, and railroad links for this prestigious event. They are also taking measures to reduce air and water pollution in the city by 2008.

Mountains and Plains

The city of Beijing is divided into four central districts: Dongcheng (East City), Xicheng (West City), Xuanwu, and Chongwen. The metropolis of Beijing, however, extends far beyond the city itself. It includes six suburban areas (Chaoyang, Fengtai, Haidian, Shijingshan, Mentougou, and Fangshan) that surround the inner urban districts. In addition, there are eight counties — Tong, Shunyi, Changping, Daxing, Pinggu, Huairou, Miyun, and Yanqing — within the metropolitan area.

With mountains in the north and west, 62 percent of the metropolis is hilly. In the far north are the Jundu Mountains and to the west the Xi Mountains. The highest point in the metropolis is Ling Shan, a 7,556-foot (2,303-meter) mountain in the far west. In contrast, the city center is flat and is about 144 feet (44 m) above sea level. To the south, the metropolis opens out into the wide, level areas of the North China Plain.

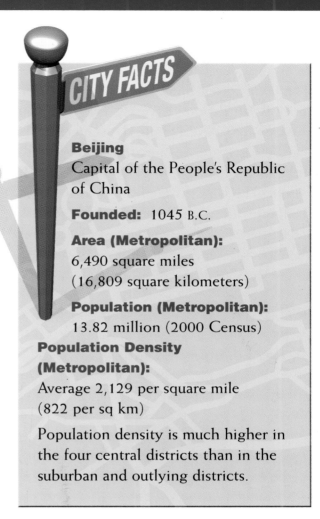

CITY FACTS

Beijing
Capital of the People's Republic of China

Founded: 1045 B.C.

Area (Metropolitan):
6,490 square miles
(16,809 square kilometers)

Population (Metropolitan):
13.82 million (2000 Census)

Population Density (Metropolitan):
Average 2,129 per square mile
(822 per sq km)

Population density is much higher in the four central districts than in the suburban and outlying districts.

Climate

Beijing has four clearly defined seasons. Winter (November to March) can be very cold with temperatures dipping as low as 1° Fahrenheit (−17.2° Celsius) and icy winds blowing from the north and northwest.

"It was filthy, beautiful, decadent, bustling, chaotic, lovable: it was the great Peking of early summer."

—Lao She, author and playwright, *Rickshaw*, 1936.
(Peking is the old Western name for Beijing.)

In spring (April to June) temperatures rise. The winds often bring sandstorms from the inner Asian deserts, covering everything in the city with dust. During the summer (July and August), the temperatures can soar to more than 104° F (40° C) and the air is humid. The winds come from the southeast, bringing afternoon thunderstorms with heavy rain. Fall (September and October) is the most pleasant season in Beijing with dry, sunny weather, warm days, and cool nights.

▼ *Tiananmen Square is the largest public square in the world. It covers an area of 100 acres (40.5 hectares) and can hold more than 1 million people.*

The Metropolis of Beijing

miles
0   50
0   50
kilometers

N

━━ Parts of The Great Wall

HEBEI PROVINCE

HEBEI PROVINCE

HEBEI PROVINCE

BEIJING METROPOLITAN AREA

Capital Airport

CITY AREA

TIANJIN PROVINCE

Earthquake Zone

On July 28, 1976, an earthquake measuring 7.8 on the Richter scale struck the city of Tangshan on the east coast of China. Over 240,000 people were killed and another 164,000 were injured. The effects of the earthquake were felt in Beijing, about 125 miles (201 km) west of Tangshan, where buildings were destroyed and there were some fatalities. Twenty-six years later, the China Museum of Popular Science and Education for the Mitigation of Earthquake Disasters opened in Beijing. Earthquakes are felt regularly in the Beijing area, so in recent years the municipal government has improved systems for monitoring and forecasting earthquakes. It has also been making plans to provide earthquake relief for stricken areas.

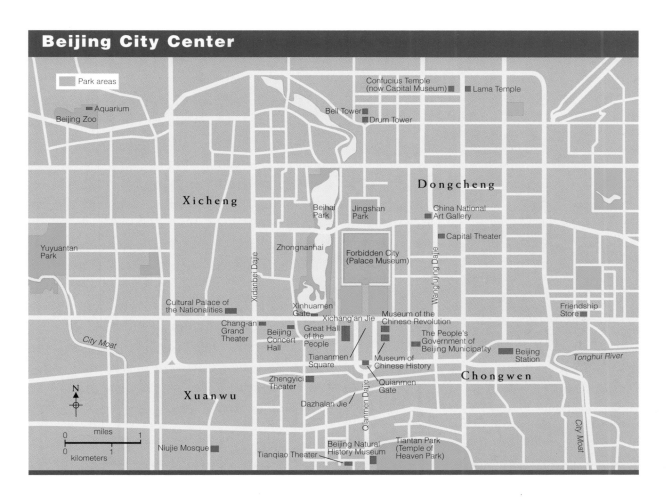

Beijing City Center

Park areas

Aquarium
Beijing Zoo

Confucius Temple
(now Capital Museum)   Lama Temple

Bell Tower
Drum Tower

Dongcheng

Xicheng

Beihai
Park

Jingshan
Park

China National
Art Gallery

Capital Theater

Yuyuantan
Park

Zhongnanhai

Forbidden City
(Palace Museum)

Wangfujing Dajie

Xidanbei Dajie

Cultural Palace of
the Nationalities

Xinhuamen
Gate

Friendship
Store

Chang-an
Grand
Theater

Beijing
Concert
Hall

Great Hall
of the
People

Xichang'an Jie

Museum of the
Chinese Revolution

City Moat

Tiananmen
Square

The People's
Government of
Beijing Municipality

Beijing
Station

Tonghui River

Museum of
Chinese History

Zhengyici
Theater

Quianmen
Gate

Chongwen

N

Xuanwu

Dazhalan Jie

Qianmen Dajie

City Moat

miles
0   1
0   1
kilometers

Niujie Mosque

Tianqiao Theater

Beijing Natural
History Museum

Tiantan Park
(Temple of
Heaven Park)

City Layout

A glance at the map above will show that, like many cities in the United States, central Beijing is laid out on a grid pattern with its main streets running north-south and east-west. This layout was established during the fifteenth century under the Ming dynasty. Its order and symmetry were based on the principles of *feng shui*, an ancient Chinese system used to determine the positioning of objects and buildings. Harmful influences were thought to come from the north, so all important buildings were situated facing south with their entrances opening toward the positive influences believed to flow from that direction. On a line running from north to south through central Beijing, some of the city's major buildings can be found: the Bell Tower, the Drum Tower, the Imperial Palace, and Tiananmen Square. The city was once enclosed by walls (now demolished) and the southern entrance, Qianmen Gate, is on the same north-south line. This was thought to be the most sacred of all the city gates and was the most elaborate.

History of Beijing

Long before recorded history, there were people living in the area now covered by Beijing. Human fossils dating back 500,000 years have been found near Beijing and there were small settlements of early farmers by about 3000 B.C. According to legend, the Xia dynasty ruled for about 600 years starting in 2100 B.C. and they founded a capital named Youzhou in the Beijing area. Under the Shang and Zhou dynasties (c.1500–1027 B.C. and 1027–221 B.C. respectively), the city developed as a trading center between the people of the hills to the north and the people who inhabited the vast central plains to the south. Under the Zhou dynasty, the city was known as Yan.

City of Many Names

In 221 B.C., Qin Shi Huangdi proclaimed himself the first emperor of China. Yan became an important administrative, trade, and military center — a position it retained for the next thousand years.

In A.D. 916, a Mongol tribe called the Khitan conquered northern China and established the Liao dynasty. Yan was renamed once more, becoming Yanjing. In the twelfth century, another nomadic tribe, the Nuzhen Tartars from Manchuria, to the

◀ *Qin Shi Huangdi, the first emperor of China, was responsible for standardizing currency, weights and measures, and the writing system across his empire.*

north of China, replaced the Liao with the Jin dynasty. They too made their capital at Yanjing, calling it Zhongdu, "central capital."

Dadu

In 1215, Genghis Khan and his Mongol horsemen swept into Zhongdu and in the battle that followed, the city was completely destroyed by fire. Under his grandson, Kublai Khan, the city was rebuilt with the Bell Tower and the Drum Tower at its center — both are still standing today. The city became the capital of the Mongol Yuan dynasty, which held power in China until 1368. Kublai Khan called his new capital Dadu, or "great capital," but in the West it was more often known by the name Khanbaliq "the Khan's city." In the thirteenth century, the Venetian explorer Marco Polo traveled to Khanbaliq and was overwhelmed by its splendor and wealth, particularly by Kublai Khan's magnificent Imperial Palace.

"You must know that this is the greatest palace ever built … The hall of the palace is so big that 6,000 people could easily eat therein … The building is altogether so wide-spreading, so rich, so beautiful that no man on earth could think of anything to outshine it."

—Marco Polo, explorer, describing the Imperial Palace in Dadu, c. 1300.

Peking Man

About 30 miles (48 km) southwest of Beijing lies the village of Zhoukoudian, where in the 1920s, the fossilized remains of ancient humans were discovered. The first finds were of teeth and jaws. A complete skullcap was unearthed in 1929. The fossils belong to Homo erectus pekinensis, *or Peking Man, and they date back approximately 500,000 years. These early humans walked upright, knew how to make fire and stone tools, hunted, and gathered nuts and berries for food.*

Ming Beijing

China returned to Chinese rule in 1368 when Ming troops conquered the Mongols. The capital of the Ming dynasty was originally established in Nanjing in the south, and Dadu was renamed Beiping, meaning "northern peace." But, in the early fifteenth century, under the Ming emperor, Yongle, Beiping once more became the capital of China and was renamed again — Beijing or "northern capital."

Between 1406 and 1420, the city was extensively rebuilt under Emperor Yongle with the Imperial Palace (the Forbidden City) at its center. Over 200,000 laborers worked on the palace, constructing huge wooden halls and marble platforms. Another impressive building of this time is the circular Temple of Heaven where the emperor went to honor his ancestors and pray for a good harvest.

▲ *The Hall of Prayer for Good Harvests, in the Temple of Heaven, dates from 1420 but was rebuilt according to the original design after partially burning down in the nineteenth century. This was the hall in which the emperor used to pray for good harvests.*

The Qing Dynasty

In 1644, China once again fell under the rule of outsiders when the Manchus, people from Manchuria, invaded and took power. They founded the Qing dynasty, which lasted until 1912. The Qing adopted Chinese styles and customs, preserving the basic structures of many of the Ming buildings. They also constructed summer palaces outside the city walls: the Old Summer Palace, Yuanmingyuan, built in the eighteenth century by Emperor Qianlong; and the New Summer Palace, Yiheyuan, built by Empress Dowager Cixi in the nineteenth century.

Western Influences

In 1793, legend says Emperor Qianlong told a British ambassador that China had no need for trade with foreigners, who he referred to as "barbarians." But, during the nineteenth century, Western demands that China open its markets to foreign goods grew stronger. The British tried to force trade with China by illegally importing the drug opium and trading it for Chinese goods. The Chinese emperors tried to stop the trade and this resulted in the Opium Wars (1839–1842 and 1858–1860). During the Second Opium War, the emperor fled from Beijing while the invading British and French troops looted and completely destroyed the Old Summer Palace at Yuanmingyuan.

The Opium Wars ended with humiliation for China, and the Europeans eventually established settlements in various parts of the country. China was also obliged to open part of Beijing to foreigners, called the Legation Quarter. In 1900, the Legation Quarter was attacked by members of the Boxers, an extremist secret society violently opposed to the foreign presence in China. After two months, the rebellion was crushed, but large parts of Beijing were devastated in the process, most notably the Hanlin Library, which was full of priceless manuscripts. The library was completely burned down.

▼ *The Old Summer Palace included many buildings of European style, where the emperor and his court ate Western food and listened to Western music.*

◄ Mao Zedong (right) attends a celebration in 1969 on the twentieth anniversary of the People's Republic of China. Lin Biao, the defense minister, is to his left.

The End of the Empire

The late nineteenth and early twentieth centuries were a time of plotting and corruption for the Manchus. The imperial family finally lost power in 1912 when the last emperor, six-year-old Pu Yi, gave up the throne. The Guomintang (the Nationalist Party), led by Sun Yat-sen, declared China a republic. However, the country was deeply divided as rival warlords fought for control. Poverty, civil war, and distrust of foreign influences led to unrest. Beijing University became a center for radical intellectuals, among them an idealistic young man named Mao Zedong. On May 4, 1919, a demonstration was held by students and intellectuals in Tiananmen Square in Beijing. They had gathered to protest the terms of the recently signed Treaty of Versailles, under which certain territories in China had been given to Japan. For many Chinese, this event sparked the beginning of the Chinese Communist movement, although the Chinese Communist Party was not founded until 1921.

During the 1920s, the Guomintang and the Communists fought together to defeat the warlords and reunite China, but in 1927, the Guomintang banned the Communist Party. In the same year, the capital of the Republic was moved south to Nanjing. Beijing was renamed, returning to its old name of Beiping. In the 1930s, China came under threat from Japan, and in 1937, Beiping fell to Japanese invaders.

The city remained under Japanese rule until the end of World War II in 1945, when the Guomintang took charge. However, the Communists had gathered support, and in 1949, they entered the city without bloodshed. On October 1, 1949, Mao Zedong proclaimed the Communist People's Republic of China from the terrace of the Gate of Heavenly Peace in

Tiananmen Square. Again, the city, renamed Beijing, was made the capital of China.

The People's Republic

The years that followed were a time of destruction for Beijing. Thousands of old buildings were torn down to make way for new development. The Communists banned religious practices and temples were turned into factories. The ancient city walls were dismantled. Only a few monuments, such as the Imperial Palace, were preserved as a showpiece of national pride. The Cultural Revolution, launched in 1966, continued the destruction of traditional Chinese culture. Mao died in 1976 and, after a power struggle, Deng Xiaoping became leader in 1978. He introduced reforms designed to modernize China. During the 1980s and 1990s, many monuments and temples in Beijing were restored and people began to enjoy a new freedom and pride in their city.

"Peking is dying. The walls are gone, the gates are gone, the arches are gone. Gone are most of the temples, the palaces, the gardens, and more and more of centuries-old Peking vanishes every day under the blows of hammers and the crushing of bulldozers."

—Tiziano Terzani, journalist and author, describing the destruction of old Beijing by the Communists after 1949.

Tiananmen Square

Tiananmen Square has been the setting for many significant events in China's history. In 1959, it was enlarged to four times its original size as the venue for mass rallies and huge parades celebrating Communism. But it has also been the place of demonstrations against the government. In April 1976, the people of Beijing gathered in Tiananmen to protest against the repression of the Cultural Revolution. In 1989, student demonstrators gathered by the thousands to demand democratic reforms. The protest (above) ended in bloodshed when soldiers and tanks moved into Tiananmen Square to break up the gathering by force. It is believed that thousands died that day, but the actual number is unknown.

CHAPTER 2

People of Beijing

There are fifty-six different ethnic groups recognized in China and people from all these groups live in the capital city. However, the vast majority of Beijing's population — about 95 percent — is Han Chinese. (The Han was an early dynasty in Chinese history and the term Han is used to describe people of native Chinese origin.) To live in Beijing, residents require government permission. However, more than 1 million people from other provinces or towns live illegally in Beijing, without this permission. They come from all over the country to look for work in the city, where there is more money and the prospects of finding work are better. The men are often employed on construction sites or do jobs such as clean public rest rooms or transport garbage. Women migrants often work as waitresses or servants. Since the reforms of the 1980s, the foreign population of Beijing has increased. These include mostly diplomats, journalists, businesspeople, and students.

Ethnic Minorities

There are about 600,000 people from ethnic minority groups living in Beijing, including Mongols and Manchus. The largest of these minority groups is made up of Chinese

◄ *Young school children visit Beijing. The long-term effects of China's one-child policy have yet to be fully assessed in China.*

Muslims, known as Hui, with a population in the city of about 200,000. The Hui come from a variety of ethnic backgrounds, including Han Chinese; their common link is that they are all followers of Islam. There are about forty mosques in Beijing. The focus for Hui life in the city, however, is Niu Jie (Ox Street) in southwest Beijing, where there are many Hui stores and restaurants as well as the Niu Jie Mosque, which dates from A.D. 966. Another Muslim minority group in Beijing is made up of Uighurs from Xinjiang in western China. The wide variety of ethnic groups in China is celebrated at the Cultural Palace of the Nationalities, located west of Tiananmen Square in Beijing. The palace houses a museum, library, auditorium, dance hall, and restaurant.

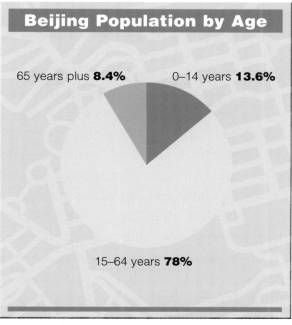

Beijing Population by Age

65 years plus **8.4%**

0–14 years **13.6%**

15–64 years **78%**

Source: www.unescap.org/pop/database/chinadata/beijing.htm

The Forbidden City

The Imperial Palace (left) lies at the heart of Beijing and was home to two dynasties of emperors — the Ming and the Qing. It was also known as the Forbidden City, because for 500 years, ordinary people were not allowed within its walls. During the Ming dynasty, this palace complex housed the emperor, his wives and concubines, and about 80,000 attendants. The huge palace covers an area of 7,750,000 square feet (720,000 sq m) and has 800 buildings with more than 9,000 rooms in all. Today, anyone can visit the Forbidden City, which has become a huge museum housing a great many art treasures.

"Little Emperors"

In 1979, the Communist government introduced a one-child policy after a period of rapid population growth both in Beijing and China as a whole. This meant that couples were allowed to only have one child; those who had more than one baby were given fines and other penalties. This policy has had some unexpected results. This "only child" generation has been given the undivided attention of parents and grandparents. Such children are called "little emperors," because they are said to be very spoiled. There have also been many cases of female babies being abandoned or even killed because families wanted a son, not a daughter, as their only child.

Religious Beliefs

The three main religions in China are Daoism, Confucianism, and Buddhism, although there are also sizeable populations of Muslims and Christians. However, centuries-old traditions of belief and worship were abruptly halted by the Cultural Revolution, when religion was banned. Many temples and monasteries were destroyed, priests were sent away, and people were prevented from worshiping. The Communist government's attitude toward religion began to relax in the late 1970s. Since then, many temples have been restored and people have begun to worship again. Today, Chinese people are officially free to worship, although the government remains suspicious of organized religion.

Daoism

Daoism is a native Chinese religion. Its founder, Laozi, is said to have lived during the sixth century B.C. *Dao* means the "way" or "path," and the central text, or book, of Daoism is the *Daodejing*, meaning "The Way and its Power." The main Daoist temple in Beijing is the Temple of the White Cloud, in the west of the city. It stands on the site of the city's first Daoist Temple, built in the eighth century A.D. During the Cultural Revolution, the temple was used as a factory, but today, its monastery houses many Daoist monks and it is the headquarters of Daoism in China. Like most of the temples in Beijing, it is actually a series of buildings separated by peaceful courtyards.

Confucius

Confucius (c. 551–479 B.C.) lived during a time of war and upheaval between rival states in China. He was a wise man who traveled the country, teaching and collecting a large band of followers as he went. Confucius believed that a ruler should set a good example for his subjects. He also stressed the importance of the family, social ties, and respect for authority. Confucianism formed the basis of government in imperial China, but in the twentieth century, the Communist government opposed Confucian ideas. Today, many Confucian temples remain closed or have been converted to other uses; for example, the large Confucius Temple in northeast Beijing is now the Capital Museum.

▲ *Originally a royal palace, the Lama Temple is made up of several halls with courtyards and gardens.*

Buddhism

Buddhism arrived in China during the first century A.D., brought from India by merchants and monks along the trade route known as the Silk Road. It spread throughout China between the third and sixth centuries, and several distinct schools of Chinese Buddhism developed. Most of the temples in Beijing are Buddhist, the best-known being the beautiful Lama Temple in the northeast of the city. This dates from the seventeenth century and is a center for Tibetan Buddhism. During the Cultural Revolution, it was closed, but under orders from the Communist president, Zhou Enlai, it was not plundered or destroyed. It reopened in the 1980s.

17

Falungong

Falungong is a movement with links to Daoism and Buddhism that uses breathing exercises as a form of meditation. It has become increasingly popular in China. The government distrusted Falungong and made it illegal for followers to demonstrate without permission. However, in April 1999, about ten thousand followers of the Falungong movement collected around the Communist government headquarters at Zhongnanhai in Beijing in an illegal demonstration. The government reacted by banning Falungong and arresting many of its members. Today, Falungong members continue to demonstrate against the Chinese government.

▼ *Traditional music and dancing are part of the outdoor celebrations that mark the Spring Festival.*

Festivals and Special Days

The festivals and special days celebrated in Beijing are a mixture of traditional, centuries-old festivities and public holidays that mark the changes brought to China since 1949. The biggest and most important traditional festival is *Chun Jie*, the Spring Festival, also called Chinese New Year, which falls some time in late January or early February. In Beijing, the Spring Festival is celebrated in parks and temples with spectacular fairs. It is also a time for families to get together and share a special meal of *jiaozi* — small dumplings filled with meat and vegetables.

Fifteen days after the Spring Festival is the Lantern Festival, when people walk through the streets of the city carrying colored paper lanterns. There are also colorful processions of musicians and dragon dancers.

Qing Ming

The ancient festival of light, Qing Ming, is also known as Tomb-Sweeping Day. In most years, it falls on April 5. It is a day to remember ancestors by cleaning their graves and leaving flowers. It is also traditional to burn paper money to ensure the ancestors' well-being in the spirit world. Today, these rituals are more common in rural areas than in modern Beijing, but in the city, children still lay flowers and wreaths in Tiananmen Square to commemorate those who died fighting for Communism.

Public Holidays

The two most important public holidays in Beijing are May 1, which is International Labor Day; and China's National Day, October 1, which celebrates the founding of the People's Republic of China. For the celebration on May 1, Beijing is decorated with flowers. Both days are marked with spectacular processions and military parades centering on Tiananmen Square. Other public holidays include International Women's Day on March 8, when women are given half a day's vacation; and National Youth Day on May 4, which commemorates the 1919 demonstrations of students and intellectuals in Tiananmen Square.

▶ *Like every Chinese festival, the Moon Festival has a special food — Moon cakes. There are many varieties, but all are round to represent the full Moon.*

Moon Cakes

The Mid-Autumn Festival, also called the Moon Festival, falls some time in September or October. This is a time for family reunions, although it is not an official public holiday. People in Beijing go out to look at the Moon and eat Moon cakes, made from a pastry crust stuffed with a variety of sweet and savory fillings. These cakes are round, to represent the full Moon, and some have a picture of Chang'e, the "Woman in the Moon," stamped onto them. According to legend, Moon cakes were used to carry secret messages during the overthrow of the Mongol Yuan dynasty in the fourteenth century.

Beverages

Tea has been drunk in China for many centuries, and today it remains the favorite nonalcoholic beverage in China. There are many different types of tea, including chrysanthemum and jasmine. Tea is drunk at home, in restaurants, and in teahouses. The main alcoholic beverage in China is beer, and Beijing has several local brands, including Yanjing and Wuxing beer. Many Chinese people also drink a strong liquor made from sorghum (Chinese sugar cane), called baijiu, and the best-selling brand, Red Star Erguotou, is made in Beijing.

▲ *Diners prepare Mongolian hot pot by plunging their choice of meat, fish, or vegetables in bubbling stock and then dipping the cooked pieces into a sauce.*

Palace and Home

For centuries, Beijing was home to the imperial court, and many of China's most famous and elaborate dishes were created for the emperor by the palace cooks, including Peking duck and bird's nest soup. Such delicacies can still be enjoyed in Beijing today at restaurants specializing in imperial cuisine, such as *Fangshan*, located in a pavilion overlooking the lake in Beihai Park.

The ordinary people of Beijing traditionally have eaten simpler food. Their diet is influenced by the city's geographical situation. Although rice is the staple food farther south in China, the climate in the north is mostly too harsh for this crop, so wheat is the main grain eaten in Beijing. Wheat has long been used to make the many types of noodles, dumplings, and bread that form the basis of a Beijing meal. Vegetables found in Beijing are those that can be grown in a northern climate — leeks, carrots, spinach, onions, garlic, and cabbages.

Beijing Specialties

Beijing is particularly famous for two dishes — Peking duck and Mongolian hot pot. Peking duck was originally an imperial dish. Many restaurants in Beijing specialize in Peking duck banquets. The duck is carefully air dried and roasted to make the skin crisp;

◄ Meat kebabs are being sold by a street vendor in Beijing. The food is cooked on a large, round pan called a wok, which is heated on a brazier — a metal basket that holds hot coals.

Eating In or Out

Most houses and apartments in Beijing have a kitchen equipped with a gas stove, but few homes have ovens. A meal at home is usually made of lots of small dishes, each freshly prepared and eaten immediately. After some cold appetizers — for example, pickled vegetables — there is often a selection of meat, fish, and vegetable dishes with noodles, rice, or steamed bread. Meals often end with a light soup.

While people most often eat traditional northern Chinese cuisine at home, restaurants across Beijing offer the chance to sample cuisine from all regions of China, including the traditional cooking of the many Chinese ethnic minorities. For example, the restaurant *Afanti* in the Dongcheng district serves Uighur food from the Xinjiang province in northwest China, including roast mutton, thick stews, and flat bread.

Western fast food is now widely available in Beijing and some of the major U.S. fast-food chains have opened there. The Chinese, however, have been producing their own kinds of fast food for centuries. Throughout the city, there are street vendors who sell traditional snacks, such as baked sweet potatoes, steamed bread, noodles, dumplings, or lamb kebabs.

it then is served with thin pancakes, spring onions, and sweet *hoisin* sauce. A true banquet starts with appetizers made with every part of the duck, including its tongue and feet, and ends with duck soup. For Mongolian hot pot, a copper pot containing boiling stock that is heated from beneath by a charcoal burner is placed in the middle of the table. Diners cook thin slices of lamb, vegetables, tofu, and noodles by plunging them into the stock, which is often made from lamb or chicken.

CHAPTER 3

Living in Beijing

Since the 1970s, Beijing has grown remarkably, with new high-rise apartment buildings, offices, and industrial plants being built around the city center. The historic center of Beijing, however, remains low rise, and there are restrictions that limit the height of new buildings in the area immediately surrounding the Forbidden City to three stories.

For centuries, most of the citizens of Beijing lived in single-story houses built around *siheyuan*, or courtyards. These houses lined the thousands of ancient alleys and lanes, known as *hutongs*, that crisscrossed the city. Beijing's hutongs date from the time the city was rebuilt after its destruction by Genghis Khan's horsemen, but houses were still being built in hutongs during the 1950s. Since then, many hutongs have been demolished to make way for modern apartment buildings, and their residents have been moved.

Courtyard Houses

The word hutong comes from the Mongolian language of the Yuan dynasty, and it probably originally meant "spring" or "well." Most of the main hutongs run from east to west, so that the main gate of each

◀ *The vast majority of the population of Beijing lives in high-rise apartment building such as this.*

▲ *Overcrowding in Beijing's hutongs, or alleyways, has led to slumlike conditions. Whether to preserve or demolish the old buildings that line the hutongs is a matter of controversy.*

Moving Out

Since 2000, more than half a million people have been moved out of "dangerous and old" housing in the center of Beijing. Typically, the amount the state pays families for their old hutong house will buy them an apartment outside the city center — where property prices are high — in one of the suburbs of Beijing. After the neighborly life of the hutong, the move to suburban living in an apartment building can be a shock. Those who make the move sometimes have to face the problems of poorer standards of schooling and longer distances to local amenities such as stores and hospitals. There can also be a sense of isolation as people who have been neighbors, often for generations, move to different parts of Beijing, and the habits of living in a community are replaced with separate, and often lonely, apartment life.

courtyard faces south. Inside the main gate, there is often a screen, or "ghost wall," to protect the courtyard from evil spirits. The courtyard usually has dwellings on all four sides, and traditionally these houses were occupied by one extended family.

Wealthy households often had more elaborate mansions with two or more courtyards with beautifully carved pillars and beams. The outer courtyard would be flanked by buildings containing the kitchen and accommodations for servants and guests. A gateway in the north wall of the courtyard led to the main courtyard, with buildings along three sides, which contained accommodations for the family.

Some houses would have another courtyard beyond this to accommodate a larger family.

During the twentieth century, many siheyuan that had previously housed just one family were adapted to accommodate four or five families, and extra houses were built in already cramped spaces. Overcrowding and a lack of adequate sanitation made for slumlike conditions in parts of the hutongs, and many of these areas have since been demolished. Today, some hutong houses are fully modernized with air conditioning, bathrooms, and full

"Great gates opened upon a vista through courtyard after courtyard, spacious, imposing. Pillared pavilions supported wide roofs that swept in stately curves against the sky. Gold leaf and lacquer and deep-cut carving made splendid the doors and pillars."

—Han Suyin, author, describing the hutong mansion of a wealthy family, 1942.

kitchens, but others remain without basic sanitation and heating. Many hutong residents still have to use a public washroom in a nearby alley, and they often have only one or two small rooms for their living space.

Modern Housing

Today, the vast majority of people in Beijing live in apartment buildings, or in large housing developments in the suburban areas of Beijing. Unlike many of the hutong houses, these new houses have running water, electricity, gas, and indoor bathrooms. The Beijing government is also trying to limit the population growth in the city's central districts by building new towns in the rural counties around Beijing.

▶ *A vendor sells calligraphic equipment on Dazhalan Street. This street is just 330 yards (302 m) long and has been a shopping center since Ming dynasty times.*

Going Shopping

Beijing has a wide range of stores and markets, ranging from huge modern malls and large department stores to traditional open-air markets and street vendors. In modern-day China, shopping is a major pastime for many people. Most stores are open from 9:00 A.M. to 8:00 P.M. daily, while open-air markets open at 10:00 A.M. and close at sunset. Prices are fixed in large department stores and other major stores, either by the government or by the owners, but elsewhere, people bargain over their purchases to get the best price.

Tongrentang

The Tongrentang Pharmacy, founded in 1669, became the imperial pharmacy for the Qing royal family in 1861. Today, the store is part of a multinational company that exports traditional Chinese medicines all over the world. Chinese remedies use many different types of herbs, as well as ingredients such as deer antlers or medicinal wine made from parts of snakes. Many Chinese people today use a mixture of traditional Chinese remedies and Western medicine.

▲ *The Dongan Department Store is typical of the large shops that have opened since the 1970s and 1980s.*

Shopping Areas

There are department stores, supermarkets, and smaller stores in all the residential areas of Beijing, but the major shopping malls in the city include those on Wangfujing, Xidan, and Qianmen Streets. Wangfujing is Beijing's main shopping street and has two huge shopping malls — the Sun Dongan Plaza and the Oriental Plaza — at either end. The street runs north to south, to the east of the Forbidden City, and it was redeveloped for the fiftieth anniversary of Communist China in 1999. Xidan lies to the west of the Forbidden City. It has long been a busy commercial quarter, with many bustling markets. Like Wangfujing, it was redeveloped and now boasts glitzy shopping malls and department stores, as well as bookstores and food markets.

Qianmen Street runs south from Tiananmen Square and the Qianmen Gate.

It is the oldest market street in Beijing, and its stores are more traditional in character, selling, for example, Chinese musical instruments, silk, and porcelain. Crossing Qianmen Street is Dazhalan Street, a small street packed with old stores, including the traditional Tongrentang Pharmacy.

The Friendship Store

Until the mid-1980s, ordinary Chinese people were not permitted to shop in the Friendship Store. This state-owned department store is located in the Jianguomenwai area of east Beijing where

▲ *Students listen attentively at a junior high school in Beijing. Education is seen as a vital tool in China's future development.*

there are many foreign embassies. Before the reforms of the 1980s, it was the only place that sold imported goods and only foreigners and Communist Party officials were allowed in. Today, it is open to everyone. It now sells Chinese products as well as many goods from overseas.

Markets

Every residential area has its own small food market, with farmers selling their own produce. Increasingly, municipal authorities are rehousing open-air markets in indoor sites. The Hongqiao market, near the Temple of Heaven in southeast Beijing, is in a shopping mall. In the basement are stalls selling food; on the first floor are household items; and on the second floor clothes, luggage, and furniture. Not far away is another well-known market, the Panjiayuan, where people go to buy crafts and antiques.

Education for the Masses

When the Communists came to power in 1949, only one-fourth of children in China attended elementary school, and only 3 percent of the population went on to high school. About 80 percent of Chinese people could not read or write. The Communist government quickly reorganized the

The Red Guards

In 1966, students at Beijing and Qinghua Universities began the Red Guard movement, which played a major part in Mao Zedong's Cultural Revolution. With Mao's backing, the Red Guards (right) attacked the four "olds": old ideas, old culture, old customs, and old habits. In practice, this meant the Red Guard physically and verbally abused anyone associated with the old ways, such as teachers and officials. Many were beaten to death. The Red Guard movement was soon joined by students from across China.

educational system to provide schooling for the masses. By 1952, 60 percent of Chinese children attended elementary school. During the Cultural Revolution, the number of hours devoted to academic learning in schools was reduced. Instead, pupils spent time doing manual labor in school gardens and workshops. From the 1950s onward, many educated young people from urban areas were also sent to rural areas to work alongside the peasants, a practice that continued until the late 1970s.

Education Now

Today, Chinese children are required to attend school for at least nine years. At three years of age, children go to local kindergartens where they play games, dance, sing, act, and learn basic language skills. Children start elementary school at the age of six, and their subjects include the Chinese language, math, and moral education. They also take part in sports and other extracurricular activities. The school day starts at 8:00 A.M., with a break for lunch between noon and 2:00 P.M. School finishes at 4:00 P.M. There are two semesters in a year — one from September to January, and one from February or March to June.

After six years, pupils move to junior high school, which lasts three years. There, they study a wider range of subjects, including history, geography, foreign languages, and sciences. Pupils can then choose whether or not to continue their education. Those who go on to senior high school study either art

"Self-discipline and Social Commitment."

—Motto of Qinghua University.

or science subjects. They study for examinations that take place at the end of senior high school, in order to gain admission to college. Others go on to specialized schools that provide training in specific subjects, such as industry, forestry, finance, or teaching. The best elementary, junior high, and senior high schools are called "key schools"; to attend them, students have to pass special tests. There are few private schools in Beijing.

Higher Education

Beijing has more than fifty centers of higher education, many of them located in the Haidian district in the northwest of the city. The most prestigious schools are Beijing University (known as Beida), founded in 1898; and Qinghua University, established in 1911. Prospective students apply to study

either the humanities or science and engineering. Those who score well on their high school examinations study at the university for three or four years and live on campus in student-run dormitories. At the moment, university education in China is free, and there are grants to help those from poor families. However, with the number of students increasing, the Chinese government is reviewing this situation. It is possible that students may have to pay for their education in the future.

Long-distance Travel

Beijing is the center of China's air, road, and railway networks. The city's Capital Airport is about 17 miles (27 km) northeast of Beijing and is the busiest airport in China. It has sixty-two international air routes and eighty-five domestic routes. It handles

Bicycles in Beijing

Most people in Beijing rely on bicycles to travel around the city (left). Many main streets are flanked on either side by bicycle lanes. With up to 8.5 million bikes on the city streets, there are special traffic wardens to control the flow of two-wheeled traffic. Large tricycles, with a platform over the back two wheels, are used to transport almost anything around the city streets — furniture, computers, or trash. There are also tricycle rickshaws that often provide a faster means of moving around the city's congested streets than a regular taxi.

▲ *Buses, cars, and red taxis fill a Beijing street.*
Traffic congestion is a continuing problem in the city.

about 35 million passengers every year. There are plans to build a third terminal at the airport because of the projected increase in passenger numbers. The railroad is also an important long-distance connector. One branch of the famous Trans-Siberian line from Moscow terminates in Beijing. There are also Trans-Mongolian and Trans-Manchurian lines, as well as a weekly train to Hanoi in Vietnam.

Local Travel

Many local trains run from Beijing's two main stations — Beijing Station and Beijing West, and from its three smaller stations. For travel around the city center, there is a small subway system with two lines. The Beijing subway is clean and efficient, and a ticket costs a standard (and small) amount of money, no matter how long or short the journey. The Loop Line has sixteen stations and follows the line of the old city wall. Line One has twenty-one stations and connects the western suburbs to the center of Beijing. The subway system is being extended as part of preparations for the Olympic Games in 2008. Line One will continue to the eastern suburbs of the city, and there will be other new lines connecting Capital Airport and the Olympic complex with the city.

Many buses and trolley cars run along the congested roads of Beijing. Bus travel is cheap, but slow, and the buses are usually very crowded. The most common form of transportation in Beijing is the bicycle, but traveling on a bike on Beijing's roads is getting more dangerous as the traffic

SARS

In the spring of 2003, a terrifying illness spread through Beijing, bringing the city to a virtual standstill. In fact, the illness, called SARS (Severe Acute Respiratory Syndrome) originated in southern China in November 2002 before being carried to Hong Kong. From there, it spread all across the world. However, the city authorities only started to admit the seriousness of the situation in Beijing in April 2003, by which time there was an epidemic in the city. The mayor and the health minister were both fired, and drastic measures were taken to bring the outbreak of SARS under control. The Beijing authorities shut down schools, placed thousands of people under quarantine, and closed theaters. They also canceled the weeklong May holiday, imposed travel restrictions, and set up roadblocks. The city was not declared free of the disease until June 2003.

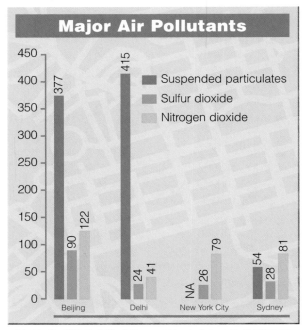

Data derived from WHO's Health Cities Air Management Information System and the World Resources Institute, collected in 1998 or, if earlier, are the latest available.

▲ *As this graph shows, Beijing is among the most polluted of the world's cities.*

volume increases. In order to cope with traffic congestion, there are four beltways around the city, with new roads due for completion before 2008.

Air Pollution

Industry and the traffic that moves slowly along Beijing's congested roads have made the city one of the most polluted in the world. Especially during the hot summer months, a thick smog (smoky fog) descends upon the city. However, as part of the preparations for the 2008 Olympics, the city government has pledged to turn Beijing into a "green" city, improving its air quality and environment in general. As part of these plans, about half of Beijing's buses already have been converted to natural gas power, which is a cleaner fuel than gasoline or diesel. Many industrial plants are being moved out of the city, freeing up land in the city center and removing industrial pollutants from the air. People are also being encouraged to use natural gas as a fuel instead of coal. All of these measures already have led to a significant improvement of air quality in the city.

Dust and Water

Every spring, sand and dust cover Beijing as huge sandstorms sweep over the city. In March 2002, a sandstorm dumped 30,000 tons (27,222 metric tons) of dust onto the city's streets. The sand, which comes from the deserts of northern China, causes respiratory problems, and people take to the streets with their faces covered by masks. The problem is that northern China's deserts have spread as trees have been cut down and land has been overgrazed, removing the layer of vegetation that held the soil in place. Since the 1980s, the city government has been working on an action plan to try to reverse these effects and reduce the number of sandstorms. Forests and other green areas have been planted to try to protect the city in the future.

The planting of trees and grass has an impact on another environmental problem in Beijing — the shortage of water. Throughout its history, the city has struggled to maintain an adequate water supply, but as the population has grown and consumption increased, the problem has become critical. There is not enough surface water from rainfall to supply the city's needs, so water is pumped to the surface from underground reservoirs. However, this is causing the general level of groundwater — the water table — to fall. The city government has responded by treating and recycling water. It is also trying to limit the amount of water that is wasted. Signs around the city urge residents to use every drop carefully.

▼ Smog hangs over Beijing. The city has pledged to reduce air pollution in time for the prestigious 2008 Summer Olympics.

CHAPTER 4

Beijing at Work

Since the time of Mao Zedong's rule, life for residents in Communist Beijing has changed considerably. The aim of Communist rule under Mao, who died in 1976, was equality for everyone, whatever work they did, and everyone in China was affected by his revolutionary ideas. When Deng Xiaoping took control in the late 1970s, he brought a different approach to Communism, with a new focus on practical results. One of his slogans was "To get rich is glorious." The change from the days of Mao could not have been more startling.

Beijing under Mao

In 1953, Mao Zedong launched an economic program known as the Five-Year Plan with the aim of achieving economic growth in China. In the countryside, land was taken away from landlords and redistributed among the peasants; in the cities, businesses were taken into state control. The main emphasis for development was on heavy industry, such as steelwork, petrochemical plants, and factories making machinery or cement. Many large industrial plants were opened in Beijing.

◄ Many heavy industrial plants were opened in Beijing during the time of Mao Zedong's rule. Mao's Five-Year Plan emphasized the development of many heavy industries to boost economic growth in China.

"Who are the people?

At the present stage in China they are the working class, the peasantry, the bourgeoisie [middle class] in the towns and throughout the country. These classes, led by the working class and the Communist Party, unite to form their own state and elect their own government.

As for the landlord class, the old government officials and civil servants… they are only allowed to behave themselves and not step out of line… If they do, they will be stopped and punished at once."

—Mao Zedong,
On the People's Democratic Dictatorship, 1949.

This rapid industrial expansion in the city quickly led to a shortage of raw materials — which often had to be imported from far away — and placed a great strain on the city's energy and water supplies. The Five-Year Plan ended in 1957 and was followed by the Great Leap Forward, a three-year plan to speed up China's economic and agricultural development. In reality, millions of people across China died from starvation as a result of Mao's Great Leap policies.

Reform

Deng Xiaoping's reforms were known as the "Four Modernizations," which targeted the areas of industry, agriculture, defense, and science and technology. Some businesses were freed from state control and private individuals were allowed to set up businesses. In the 1980s and 1990s, the policy of encouraging heavy industry in Beijing was brought to an end. Instead, the municipal government began to concentrate on promoting the city as the political, cultural, and economic center of China. Many industrial plants were relocated outside the city. In their place, light industries such as electronics, food processing, and printing were set up. An increasing number of stores and restaurants opened across the city.

Foreign Investment

Between 1949 and 1960, the Soviet Union helped China develop its industries and cities through grants, loans, and investments. But apart from this aid from a fellow Communist state, there was no foreign investment in China and little trade with other countries under Mao. This, too, began to change as part of Deng's reforms. Many Chinese students were sent to Western universities to study subjects such as science and engineering. Western companies were encouraged to invest in Chinese enterprises. Since the 1980s, many foreign financial institutions and companies have established bases in Beijing, and in 2002, it was estimated that about 158 of the world's top 500 companies had headquarters there, many of them linked to high-tech industries.

The result of Deng Xiaoping's reforms was steady economic growth throughout the 1980s and 1990s. Between 1981 and 1991, the amount of China's exported goods multiplied five times, and foreign investment coming into the country was multiplied by four, despite problems caused by the aftermath of the demonstrations in Tiananmen Square in 1989. In the late 1990s, a financial crisis swept across Southeast Asia, hitting the booming economies of Japan and Korea very hard. However, China survived this crisis and is seen as one of the East's key large economies in the twenty-first century.

Rich and Poor

While many of Beijing's businessmen and women can afford expensive cars and other luxury items, life is often not so good for the ordinary worker. Millions of people continue to work for state-owned industries, many of which are undergoing radical reform in order to make them profitable. This usually involves cutting back on the workforce, and many people are being laid off — in 2001 alone, over 5 million people were laid off from state-owned businesses across China. Only one-third of this number found new employment. The rest must rely on basic state unemployment benefits to survive. Unemployment is hitting rural workers and urban workers alike, and millions of people have moved to the cities illegally to look for work.

Beijing's "Silicon Valley"

Northwest of the city is Zhongguancun, an area known as Beijing's "Silicon Valley" (after the "Silicon Valley" in California). It is home to the Chinese Academy of Sciences as well as many other research institutions. It is also the location of many high-tech companies (below). The companies make and sell almost anything to do with computers. For the people who work in Zhongguancun, technology is one of the brightest hopes for future economic growth.

Main Industries

Despite its problems, Beijing is a city looking to the future. It still has some heavy industries, such as an oil refinery and a steel factory, but light and high-tech industries have become very important to the city. Service industries are big employers, too. These are industries providing people with a service rather than a product, such as banking, insurance, and tourism. There are

▲ Traditional crafts, such as cloisonné work, are still practiced in small factories in Beijing. To make cloisonné, wire is soldered to a metal object — a vase in this picture — to form the outlines of a pattern. Enamel is then put into the spaces between the wires, and the object is fired several times in a kiln.

also smaller companies making traditional goods, including lacquerware (objects coated with a decorative finish of a natural

▲ *The Great Hall of the People, on the west side of Tiananmen Square, is the headquarters of China's parliament — the National People's Congress.*

substance called lacquer), carvings in jade, and cloisonné work (metal and ceramic objects decorated with enamelwork). There is some agriculture within metropolitan Beijing, but most food for the city is grown in its surrounding rural counties.

The City Government
Beijing is an independent municipality in the Hebei province, one of four independent municipalities in China. It is governed by the Beijing People's Congress, which is in turn controlled by the Chinese Communist Party. The party controls the appointment of people to senior positions, such as mayor and secretary in the congress. The party also exerts control over the many departments in the Beijing People's Congress, such as urban planning, family planning, foreign trade, and commerce. The People's Congress meets in chambers in the Great Hall of the People on the western side of Tiananmen Square. There are more than seven hundred

Beijing's Underground World

In 1969, work started on a vast tunnel system beneath Beijing. Mao Zedong launched the project with the slogan "Dig tunnels deep. Store grain everywhere. Be ready for natural disaster and war!" The reason for the tunnels was fear of nuclear war with the Soviet Union. Entrances into the tunnels were built everywhere — in schools, stores, and factories, as the tunnels were intended to be a means of escape for the people of Beijing. The tunnels were dug by hand by volunteers, and the work continued until 1979. With the fear of nuclear attack at an end, this "underground world" has been adapted for other purposes. Some tunnels today form part of the subway system; others are stores and restaurants.

members of the congress, and they elect the city government for a term of five years. Ordinary people have the right to vote for members of the congress but not for the officials of the Communist Party.

National Government

Beijing is also the home of the national government and the Chinese Communist Party. The Great Hall of the People is China's parliament building, where the three thousand or so representatives of the National People's Congress meet for two or three weeks every year. The congress has the power to pass laws, amend the constitution, approve economic plans and national budgets, and to appoint members of the State Council — the central governmental body or cabinet, led by the Chinese premier.

The most powerful positions of authority in the government of China, however, are those of the premier and general secretary of the Communist Party. China is a communist state and has only one official political party. Top members of the Communist Party have residences and offices in Zhongnanhai, just west of the Forbidden City. In fact, this compound is known to Beijing residents as the new "Forbidden City," as ordinary citizens and foreign visitors are not permitted to enter it.

The name Zhongnanhai means "Central and Southern Lake," and the complex is built around two lakes that once formed part of a pleasure garden for the imperial court. After imperial rule ended in 1912, it was used as the presidential palace. Today, the compound includes living quarters, a grand reception hall, and a meeting hall for leading party members, known as the Politburo. Also within the compound is the traditional courtyard villa of Mao Zedong. His rooms are kept as they were during his lifetime, with some of his personal belongings on display.

The main entrance to Zhongnanhai, called Xinhuamen (New Flowery Gate) is guarded by two soldiers and has been the site of many demonstrations, notably by protesting students in 1989 and followers of Falungong in 1999.

CHAPTER 5

Beijing at Play

During the Cultural Revolution, the arts came under the control of Mao Zedong's wife, Jiang Qing. The only performances permitted in the theaters and movie houses were plays, ballets, or movies that celebrated the revolution and its heroes. Since the death of Mao, these restrictions have been lifted and entertainment in Beijing has slowly come back to life.

Theaters, Movies, and Concerts

Theatergoing is a popular pastime in Beijing, and there are several theaters to choose from. These include the Capital Theater and the theater at the Central Academy of Drama. Plays by Western playwrights are performed in translation, as well as plays by Chinese authors such as Lao She, who wrote the famous *Teahouse* (1958), a play set entirely in a Beijing teahouse. Going to movie houses is also popular in China, particularly to see action-packed martial arts movies. The Chinese government controls the number of foreign movies released in China, and these are shown at a few movie houses in Beijing.

Concerts of both Chinese and Western classical music are held at the Beijing

◄ *An acrobat performs a balancing act on top of some chairs. Acrobatic performance is an ancient Chinese art form that combines strength and grace.*

Beijing Opera

Beijing Opera (left) is a unique art form. It is about two hundred years old, although its main elements — song, dance, mime, and acrobatics — date back many centuries. It started when troupes from the Anhui and Hebei provinces came to Beijing to perform for the imperial family in the late eighteenth and early nineteenth centuries. It soon became the favorite entertainment for people of all levels of society. The stories performed within Beijing Opera come from Chinese legend, folktales, and history. During the Cultural Revolution, all of these subjects were banned, and only eight "model plays" about the class struggle of the revolution were permitted. These restrictions were lifted in 1978, and performances of traditional Beijing Opera resumed. Today, Beijing Opera is performed nightly at the restored Zhengyici Theater, the Huguang Guild Hall, and the Chang'an Grand Theater, as well as other venues in Beijing.

Concert Hall, or the concert hall in the Forbidden City. At other venues around the city, there is live music every night that caters to all tastes, including rock music at the Sound Stage and jazz at the CD Café. Discos and karaoke bars are also popular among Beijing's young people.

Acrobatics and Puppet Shows
More traditional forms of entertainment include opera, acrobatics, and puppet theaters. The tradition of acrobatic performance extends back over two thousand years in China. The feats performed by groups such as the Beijing Acrobatics Troupe are breathtaking to watch and performances can be seen at the Wan Sheng Theater and the Universal Theater. Traditional puppet plays are performed at the China Puppet Theater using both glove and shadow puppets. Performances are popular with both children and adults.

Museums and Art Galleries
When the Communists defeated the Nationalist Guomintang in 1949, the defeated leaders fled to Taiwan where they set up an alternative Chinese Republic. They took with them many of Beijing's most valuable treasures, which are now on display in the National Palace Museum in Taipei. Many other cultural relics were destroyed during the Cultural Revolution. Today, the Chinese government is trying to recover,

renovate, or replace lost items wherever possible, to fill the gaps left by the looting and destruction.

Beijing's largest and most magnificent museum is the Forbidden City, officially called the Palace Museum. Visitors to its huge halls and courtyards can see where the emperor and his court lived, view items such as the magnificent Dragon Throne, and witness the wealth of the Imperial Treasury. Nearby, in Tiananmen Square, the Museum of Chinese History and the Museum of the Chinese Revolution document China's history. At the northern end of Wangfujing Street, the China National Art Gallery showcases contemporary Chinese artists. It also displays more traditional Chinese art and has occasional exhibitions of foreign art.

▲ *The Dragon Throne in the Forbidden City is located in the Hall of Supreme Harmony. It is from there that the emperors ruled China.*

Out and About

Every morning, people go to Beijing's parks and open spaces to practice martial arts such as *taiji* and *qigong*. Many others choose to start the day with a game of chess or by taking their pet birds out for a walk in their cages. Other popular outdoor pastimes include badminton, ping pong, kite flying, and ballroom dancing. Outdoor swimming is popular in places such as Kunming Lake at the Summer Palace. During the cold Beijing winters, ice skating is possible on the frozen waters of the lake.

For trips in town, people can visit the Beijing Zoo, where the main attraction is

▶ *Much of the Great Wall of China had fallen into decay until, in 1984, Deng Xiaoping launched a campaign to "Love China, Restore the Great Wall." Today, it is China's main tourist attraction.*

the giant pandas; or the Beijing Aquarium, in the northeastern corner of the zoo. Alternatively, many people have a picnic in one of the city's many green spaces, such as Beihai Park, or the Summer Palace.

Out of Town

Not only are there are many fascinating places to visit within the Beijing metropolis, there is much to see outside the city as well. The most obvious of these attractions, and the one that receives the most visitors, is the Great Wall. The nearest section, and therefore the most crowded, is in Badaling, about 35 miles (56 km) northwest of Beijing. Another popular destination is the Ming Tombs, about 30 miles (48 km) northwest of the city. Thirteen of the sixteen Ming emperors were buried there and the biggest of the tombs is that of Emperor Yongle.

Also to the northwest of the city, and just beyond the Summer Palace, lies Xiang Shan (Fragrant Hill Park). This beautiful area, set in the Western Mountains, was once the imperial game reserve where emperors went to hunt animals, such as tigers. Today, it is open to everyone and many Beijing residents love to go there to escape the city crowds — especially in the fall when the leaves of the maple trees covering the mountains are a blaze of red color.

"It [the Great Wall] perched like a cardboard cut-out upon mountains... undeterred by precipices. Cold stone blocks... bound by crumbly mortar, lay chalky white and friable at the side of the parapet, as if left by workmen just days ago..."

—William Lindesay, author and travel writer, *Alone on the Great Wall*, 1989.

CHAPTER 6

Looking Forward

The biggest upcoming event for Beijing is the 2008 Olympic Games. About $3.2 billion will be spent on the construction of the Olympic venues themselves. The Beijing metropolitan government has also pledged to improve the city's infrastructure and environment in time for the games, and so $21.6 billion has been set aside to tackle these problems.

The construction of the Olympic venues is slated for completion by 2006, to allow time for testing and any extra work that needs to be done. These venues will include a new 80,000-seat National Stadium, a 19,000-seat arena, a 20,000-seat cultural and sports center, and a 17,000-seat swimming pool arena. Many training and support facilities will also be built, including an international broadcast center and an Olympic Village providing housing, training, and leisure facilities for the athletes and their coaches.

The Changing Face of Beijing

All of this modernization means that Beijing is changing fast — too fast for some. Many people are becoming increasingly concerned about the wholesale demolition of historic Beijing, particularly its hutongs. Only fifty years ago, Beijing had about

◀ *One week after this picture was taken (on July 3, 2001), Beijing was chosen to host the 2008 Olympics.*

▲ *Modern office buildings in Beijing show how much the city has changed since the 1970s.*

Water Crisis

One of Beijing's biggest issues for the future is the city's water supply. Ambitious plans are being made to build three massive canals that will bring water to the capital from the Yangzi River and its tributaries in the south of China. Water from this source could be on tap in Beijing by 2010. However, it is estimated that between 30 and 40 percent of the city's water escapes into the ground from broken pipes. Many experts argue that repairing these pipes is a more pressing necessity than bringing water over long distances. They also say that only when Beijing residents pay a realistic price for their water will they start to take the water shortage problem seriously.

3,200 hutongs; today, only 990 remain. Many Beijing citizens fear that the demolition of these hutongs means the disappearance of a whole period of history and culture in the life of their city. The problem for the city government is how to preserve and renovate the shabby, but historically valuable, hutongs, while at the same time trying to build a cosmopolitan, modern metropolis.

In the meantime, many new building projects, environmental improvement plans, and various schemes to make the city a better place to live indicate that Beijing is determined to present itself to the world as a truly twenty-first century city.

"New Beijing, Great Olympics."

—Motto of Beijing Olympics, 2008.

Time Line

c. 3000 b.c. There are small settlements of farmers in the Beijing area.

221 b.c. Qin Shi Huangdi proclaims himself first emperor of China.

a.d. 916 The Khitan establish the Liao dynasty.

1125 The Nuzhen Tartars replace the Liao with the Jin dynasty.

1215 Genghis Khan destroys Beijing, then called Zhongdu.

1267 Kublai Khan starts to reconstruct Beijing, then called Dadu.

1368 The Mongols are overthrown and the Ming dynasty is founded.

1406–1420 Beijing is rebuilt around the new Imperial Palace.

1644 The Manchu Qing dynasty is founded.

1839–42 The First Opium War is fought.

1858–60 The Second Opium War is fought and ends with the destruction of the Summer Palace in Beijing.

1900 The Boxer Rebellion is crushed.

1912 The Qing dynasty and imperial rule ends.

1921 The Chinese Communist Party is founded.

1937 Beijing, then called Beiping, falls to Japanese invaders.

1945 World War II and the Japanese occupation come to an end.

1949 Mao Zedong declares the creation of the People's Republic of China in Beijing.

1953 Mao Zedong launches the Five-Year Plan.

1958–61 The Great Leap Forward, aimed at improving China's agriculture and economy, causes many to die of starvation instead.

1966 The Cultural Revolution begins.

1976 Mao Zedong dies; the Tangshan earthquake strikes.

1978 Deng Xiaoping becomes the new Chinese leader.

1989 Tiananmen Square demonstrations end in death for Chinese students when their protest is crushed by the Chinese government.

1999 Falungong demonstrations take place in Beijing and many protesters are arrested.

2003 The SARS illness strikes Beijing.

2008 Beijing will host the Olympic Games.

Glossary

Boxers members of a Chinese extremist organization, formed at the end of the nineteenth century, that attacked and killed foreigners wherever they could.

Buddhism religion that follows the teachings of the "Buddha" (the "Enlightened One"), seeking peace and an end to suffering through living a pure and simple life.

Communism a political system that aims to create a society in which everyone is equal. One of its central principles is the communal ownership of all property.

Confucianism a Chinese philosophy that is based on the teachings of Confucius (551–479 B.C.). Confucian thought stresses the importance of family ties, social ties, and respect for authority.

Cultural Revolution a movement started by Mao Zedong in 1966 that attacked the four "olds": old ideas, old culture, old customs, and old habits. Schools and universities were closed, and many people were beaten or killed. The revolution ended with the death of Mao in 1976.

Daoism a Chinese religion founded by Laozi, who is said to have lived during the sixth century B.C. Daoists think that humans are part of the natural world and that they should live in harmony with nature by keeping the two opposing forces of *yin* and *yang* in balance.

dynasty the ruling family of a country over several generations.

Falungong a religious movement with Buddhist and Daoist links that uses breathing exercises as a form of meditation.

feng shui means literally "wind, water" and is an ancient Chinese system used to work out how buildings and monuments should be positioned. It is based on the principle that an invisible energy, called "*qi*," flows through and around us and that balancing the two aspects of this energy (yin and yang) is important for a healthy and successful life.

Guomintang The Chinese Nationalist Party, founded by Sun Yat-sen in 1919. The Nationalists fought the Communists for control of China.

Han an early dynasty in Chinese history. The term is also used to describe people of native Chinese origin.

hutong the lanes and alleys that run between traditional courtyard houses in older areas of Beijing.

karaoke entertainment in which people sing along to prerecorded backup music.

nomadic describes people who move from place to place, with no fixed settlement.

Opium Wars (1839–1842 and 1858–60) two wars fought between China and Britain over trading rights, particularly with reference to the drug opium. China was defeated in both wars and was forced into trade concessions.

qigong a martial art involving breathing and physical exercises. The aim of qigong is to balance yin and yang forces in the mind and the body.

quarantine when people are forced to live in isolation for a set period of time, to prevent the spread of an infection that they may be carrying.

Red Guards a student movement that started at Beijing University in 1966 and played a major part in the Cultural Revolution. With the official blessing of Mao Zedong, these student activists attacked anything that was "old," including authority figures such as teachers.

rickshaw a two- or three-wheeled passenger vehicle powered by a cyclist.

SARS (Severe Acute Respiratory Syndrome) a pneumonia virus that originated in southern China in 2002 and spread around the world. It affected Beijing particularly badly in Spring 2003.

siheyuan a courtyard with single-story houses on all four sides. Such courtyards are traditional in Beijing.

taiji (t'ai chi) a martial art that involves shadow boxing.

Treaty of Versailles The treaty that was drawn up after the end of World War I, under which territories in China that had belonged to Germany were given back, not to China, but to Japan.

trolley car a trackless bus powered by an electric current that is transferred from a pair of overhead wires.

Further Information

Books
Baldwin, Robert F. *Daily Life in Ancient and Modern Beijing (Cities Through Time)*. Runestone Press, 1999.

DuTemple, Lesley A. *The Great Wall of China*. Lerner Publications, 2003.

Hatt, Christine. *Beijing (World Cities)*. Thameside Press, 1996.

Hatt, Christine. *Mao Zedong*. World Almanac, 2003.

Kent, Deborah. *Beijing (Cities of the World)*. Children's Press, 1999.

Le Bas, Tom. *Insight Guide: Beijing (Insight City Guides)*. Langenscheidt Publishers, 2000.

Web sites
www.curiouskids.com/beijing_facts.htm
Information about Beijing and a language guide.

www.mondovista.com/china33.html
Answers to many questions kids ask about China.

http://www.beijing-olympic.org.cn
The web site for the 2008 Olympic Games.

http://www.unesco.org/ext/field/beijing/whc/pkm-site.htm
Information about the Peking Man.

http://www.chinavista.com/experience/tiananmen/main.html
Information about Tiananmen Square in Beijing.

english.bjta.gov.cn/about/index.asp
Lots of information about all aspects of Beijing, including its history, environment, and food.

Index